The fig

Gus is on the log.

Gus runs to the bin.

Gus hits the bin.

The bin tips on to the log.

Gus hops up on the log.

Gus gets on top of the bin.

Gus gets the fig!

The fig

Level 2, Set 2: Story 11

Before reading

Say the sounds: g o b h e r f u l

Practise blending the sounds: fig Gus log runs bin hits tips up gets top hops

High-frequency words: a on **Tricky words:** the is to of
Vocabulary check: tips – to tip something is to tilt it or knock it over. We say "I tip" but "He tips".

Story discussion: What do you think Gus the greedy goat will do when he sees a big ripe fig on a tree?

Teaching points: Check that children can say the phonemes /g/ /o/ /b/ /h/ /e/ /r/ /f/ /u/ /l/, and that they can identify the grapheme that goes with each phoneme. Check that they can remember the sequence of events in the story.
Check that children can identify and read the tricky words: the, is, to, of. Introduce tricky words "of" and "to". Note that "f" makes a /v/ sound and "o" makes an /oo/ sound.

After reading

Comprehension:
- Where does Gus see the fig?
- How does he feel when he sees it?
- How do you think the owner of the bin would feel about what Gus does?
- Can you remember all the things Gus does to try to reach the fig?

Fluency: Speed-read the words again from the inside front cover.